Dream Your Dream

Deborah Brooks Langford

Dream Your Dream

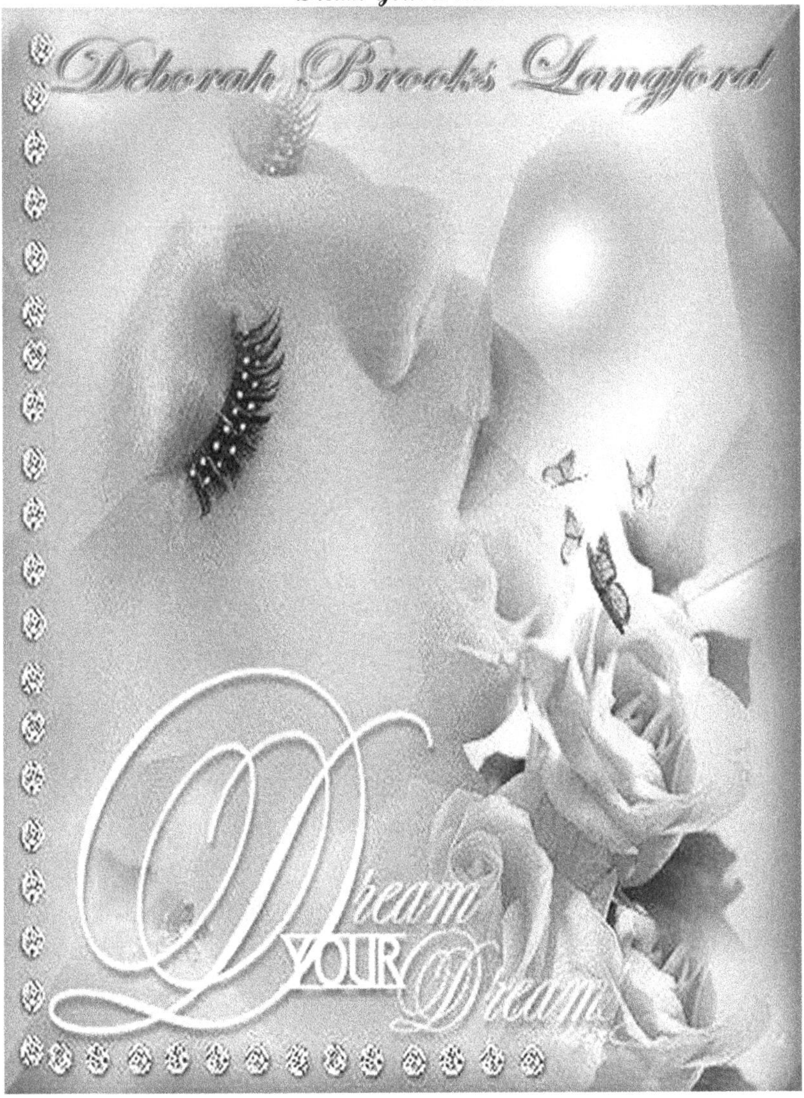

Graphics by Susan Joyner Stumpf

Dedication Page

I want to thank all my poetry and authors friends
For Dreaming their Dreams
And never give up
God bless you all..

Your ISBN:
978-1-304-64309-4

Contents I

Contents II

Another Hidden Day

A distance in the night
I saw you but a glimpse
We once were so right...
It was another hidden day
As my restless mind wandered
In dreams of you..
Your velvet kiss was there
Your fingertips down my back
Your heated gaze singeing...
Lovers soot upon my skin
A forbidden, sweet, nonsensical
Magical sin...
My wanting overwhelms me
Remembering our secret,
Clandestine day dream...
You my desperate addition,
Tears my conscience to shreds
Can you hear me screaming....
There you were in my hidden day
You saw my tears and you turned away
Why can't I have you, my hidden love.....
When I close my eyes, there you are
Just like before
In my hidden days
Anges écrire dans le ciel
Angels Wmots simples ils ne écrire des mots
D'amour que serenade
Métissage, sur la
Musique breeze tombe pleurant
Murmure d'amour
À suivre la lecture de la berceuse
De leur chère notes
Par les anges, qui écrit dans
Le ciel...
Leur beauté en porcelaine
Pour tous à voir
Oblige une swift stride
Qui ne peut cacher
Qu'ils partagent leur coeur
En vol ludique
Qu'ils écrivent dans le ciel...

Angels Write In The Sky

Simple words they do write
Words of love that serenades
Mingling, on the breeze
Music falls weeping
Whispering of love
To follow the lullaby
From their cherished notes
By the angels,
Writing in the sky....
Their porcelain beauty
For all to see
Compels a swift stride
That cannot hide
They share they hearts
In playful flight
As they write in the sky...

Our Hearts Whisper

Our hearts sustain our souls
Breathes in us life
As our whispers carries our spirits
To flight
As we close our eyes
And feel the love of the other
Touching our skin
Seducing our minds
Serenading our hearts
As you physically alter me….

The unleash beauty
With a softly hushed motif,
Changing nuance and color
As it passes our lips…

Our quiet declaration,
Like a salty lullaby
Raises excitement
Along our heated skin
You keep me wanting
Needing
Things I never knew I could have
Our whispers is a touch,
A passionate explorer
Mapping out our bodies
Legs wrapping and draping
Like passionate explorers that we are…
Your light heated breath excites me
Roaming
Around me,
You raise me up
From ash cinders
To combustive flame
Beneath your brush
As you engulf me
Like s melody I soften
Into you

You're my favorite song
As you whisper my name...
Our Hearts whisper
Each other's souls
As you mouth your needs in my ear
Caressing my heart to a staggering beat
I feel everything on a hushed caress
As it caress kisses to my soul...
I shiver with our lovers secret that
Is only for me...

I Listen For the Door

I sit here in the middle of nothing
Reaching and reaching for the end
Now that you are gone, it has been very long....

Moving images, oblique surroundings dim my senses
Tears flow to the scheme of things
Nothing will ever be the same
Since death took you in its strides...

You're healing embrace and the pose of your mind
Your strong will, took no prisoners
Our journey as lovers kept me captive
Shattered... shuddering, trembling
Tears racked my very soul...

My cherished lover, in passion and dreams
As I sit here and listen for the door..

Masked Lover

The ball was on, in full swing
Hypnotic, blinding prisms of light
With gathered glass floating peering
With blurred sight
Until the masked lover appeared that night
Her aching soul naked before all, was bored to the tee
Gentle fingers tilted each face.... They were on bended knee
Never seen the lights of the masked lover...
A shadow, a face, a vision of lust
Gathering what's left of the final destruction
Shattered on the floor hearts and more hearts
Galore
Heart of stone she saw them bleed
Hopeless, unfix able desperate to be
Her feather touch leaning toward the withered
Bodies
As her naked soul peered through the night
With broken hearts crying out loud
A strange amber fog floats in above their heads
A crow swoops out to devour her eyes..
The masked Lover had a good time
Breaking hearts leaving destruction as she laughed
What a great night she had, until the crow ate her soul....

Dream Your Dreams

I want to fly in the wind
Can't you hear my thoughts screaming?
I want to write, and love
All others just leave me alone....
My desperate addiction,
You are...
I solemnly toss my wishes to you
As I write,
All others just leave me alone...
The music plays as I paint my canvas
And there you are
My desperate addiction
Take me with you on your journey
To never - never land
Open the door now
As I knock so urgently
You are my sweet forbidden dream
My magical sin…..
Open up my favorite wine
Sit with me in front of the fire
Read to me your favorite poetry
Kiss me one last time
My desperate Addiction...

Just Close Your Eyes

Let me make love to you in the coolness,
Where our souls exchange wisdom
Where you live inside my eternity
Where you wash away my tears....
You reach for me way down deep
Hold my hunger of you in your hands
As my voracious hunger steals yours
You say... 'Just close your eyes'...
We explore our love with whispers
Desires that weaken my knees
My love... let me be your addition
You say.. '
Shhhh, Just close your eyes...'
Let me lay kisses on your chest
Your mouth press against mine,
Softy at first we lay,
Open to mimic the artful art of Love
That our night dreams replay...'
Just close your eyes...'
Let me paint you a masterpiece
Look carefully to my canvas
As I sleep into your subconscious
Colors bleed you through to me...
'Shhhhh, my love, just close your eyes."

Dreams are Sublime

Pondering thoughts awaken her, stirring of echoes past
Tears do stream violently deep within her soul....

She makes love to him so many different ways
Dreams of fantasy from her to him, vision of love around every corner
With dreams that gives her, his power....

He kisses her in her daydreams, he holds her tight at night
Awakening to the thoughts of reality, makes her want to cry....

With a tear in her eye, she whimpers let me sleep
As he kisses her sweet giving lips, as the tip of her petal melts...

Simple creatures are they, following loves intimacy
She beckons him come, like a wounded dove...

I Know Sorry Isn't Enough

Jagged edge sword, penetrates deep
Slicing skin as words cuts the very soul
Stomach turns and twists, brain cluttered
With thoughts
Of you
Torment is controlling comes smashing in my dreams
Wanting to be held in this darkening fall...
With the pain comes fear of always being alone....
Had we met in the past life, would I had been invisible
As I search my lonely heart and caress my very soul
And I want you no matter what...
Daydreaming of you comes daily
Just waiting for my eyes to close so I can see your face...
Walking the dirt road, I look left then right
Wondering which way to go, are you my new journey or left behind...
I make my first step, and a warm breeze blows my hair
Flying around my head, and I wonder...
Which way do I go???

My Dream of You

I woke up one morning in a village of shadows
You were standing there, your hand outstretched
A smile so dreamy...
The north rising sun, was melting our hearts
My eyes could not fathom, the want in your eyes
You had a spell on my soul....
Darkness emerges; I am pulled from my resting place
As I felt your hands and your love arms; your warm breath
Controlling my every need...
A lovers kiss, rests on my lips. Dances across me for miles
Dark heat blooms in my belly, it pushes through me still
As currents rush through my veins;
Nourishing my spirit with your love, as I surrender
So tenderly…...Coming with you, to that glorious place
Where nothing else matters...
My arms are outstretched, searching and wanting the need of you
For, you are not there. And then I remember, this is only a dream,
A dream in vivid color, a glorious dream of you....

A Beauty to See

Blue Ocean is serenity,
Beneath depths is a mystical company that is divine...
Dancing bodies' transference,
Like anemones secrets, to the sway of mystical creatures...
She was the Maid of the Seas they called her
A beauty to see, flowing ribbons, hair floating in a silken collage...
Her caressing silky skin, ripened with the very touch
The prince from Prussian Waters losing control in his arms...
Pending, driving rain rush upon the seas that fateful night
Strength enveloped her, from her watchful rugged guardian....
Mysterious, emotional paradox in the turbulent storm
Gentle, in the core he cherishes her love her him, her magnificent, man....
Tenderness in his outstretched arms, keeping her safe from the storm
The twisting storm eager, to grab just one last victim, longing to be adored
She loves him with all of herself, this beautiful Maid of the Sea
Her prince with untamed passion that held the stars, untamed....
Seeing through the darkness with unlimited heart songs
Sang his last song, on her lips, as the storm took his life that very night...

Another Breath

Another breath I breathe when I think of you
Another dream I dream with you full color
Night after night, I revise our dream set....
Just a fortnight ago...I saw us strolling hand in hand
We were wandering souls, searching for the other
No ties, only love...
We halted beneath the brightest moon of fantasy
Our lips collide in mated frenzy...
As long as my lashes land on your heated face
My lonesome hands wandering, as your fingers are adoring....
While I trace your face, neck, and chest
I am beguiled by our dreams state exploration....
I raise high on the drug of your whispering lines
Never seeking sobriety...
Of course I wake alone to the morning lights
Remembering the breath of you, my man...

I Saw Your Picture Today

I saw the blue of your eyes
A glimpse here and there
A vision maybe...
A flickering, of the silhouette rush
Of colors, that blinded me to you....
I saw your picture today
And my mind saw the glorious sun
Of a man that I wanted more
Than you would ever know...
Remembering us,
Sitting in the middle of the floor
Before a roaring fire... with my poems in hand
Reading each word softly, with your lips
Pressings mine in between each ghostly recollection...
Now your picture
Are haunting, sitting pressed upon my mind
Pressing haunts of your dreams....
I still love you...
It was a paradise...

Hello Mom

Dear Mom
I know you went to heaven
I know you are with all the Angels
The beauty of your soul
And Was all knowing

My angel, my mom....

You always told me how you loved me
How proud you were of your daughter
You loved me like no other
Could love....

Mom, I sit here looking out the window
So glad you are not in pain
So glad you touched my heart
Like only an Angel could....

But mom I still cry, I miss you so much
Dear Mom, how could I compare
As a mom like you had been?
You were the most wonderful mother
And yes I am trying to behave, so mom I could see you
One of these many days...

Good bye for now my sweet mom
Goodbye is such sweet sorrow
So instead I say, hello my mom
One day soon it will be....

Love Your Daughter...

Romeo, Romeo Where for Art Thou My Love

There you are my Romeo
But there is no light
Do not leave my side, my love...
There is no light, this night
On a subtle kiss of the moon on your lips
There are the shadowed lines of our lives
In design, my eyes strain to see my Romeo, my love...
Feeling his hand on each side
His face leans close
She tastes his breath
There is no love, like the love of him......
In a frantic rush their mouths collide
And swell in mutual hunger
In a blazing greed to feel skin to skin
Under a sculptors masterful hands
Lips that follow restless hands
Laying velvet caresses
Along her throat that trembles
Under his kiss
Romeo, my Romeo, where forth art there,
My lover, my life....

And Still I Write

And Still As I sat at my desk,
Remembering the water fall
Remembering you...
My muse rambled on and on,
I could not stop my words as they folded to you my love.
My sin...
Showed one more time as I struggled with your touch
You hid my heart in the winds of your world,
You found the tears on my cheek.
You never asked me what was wrong.
Then you were gone,
This makes me cry
To find you so unconcerned for my safety
And so I write.....
But Darling your love makes me melts like rain,
Our starving moon that weeps and weeps for our love to be
Is lost one more time...
Why don't you love me anymore?
You kept asking me and wanting my love
I gave you all of me
But the blessings are few unless I am in your arms
That's where the sin comes in
I don't want just a dream,
But your frozen magic that stills holds my destiny
My heart that bleeds crimson magic and even despair....
Dear love...
I want your love your special touch that finds my soul,
That holds my tears in your eyes,
That kisses my breath in your mouth.
My breasts long for your matador,
And the moon at our backs,
Hiding your hands,
Holding me in your embrace
With lavender folding around our bodies,
Kissing the dew of tears one last time...
Oh darling,
How you rained down on me slowly in poetry
Now snow white rays of clarity that shows
That bed of river flowing in our quietude here..
I love you darling,
Oh so much....

Into me you bleed and moan,
Our bed is on an edge of gold....
As our love in the rain,
That dropped millions of drops of you,
Falling all around my body and kissing my body so new,
Holding this side of light with sweet stars so bright
Yes those millions of drops of rain,
That falls on our bodies, as your kisses explore,
The image is brought forward in my dreams as I lay so spellbound
Forevermore
Hello my love,
My darling,
I am curious to see how your heart is holding up?
Seeing you standing there,
Looking so grand in your black suit,
As I watch you... I realize that my tears don't affect you anymore...
The sound of your breathing don't become you,
Although I know, it was the purest divine love that we had,
That was turning the wheel with divine blessings.
It was a thousand high souls that night,
That I wrote,
With a million drops of you,
Falling like rain between my life and yours.
Then I looked at the rays of midnight sun...
Yet you are gone now...
What did I do wrong?
And I still write...
I Write

Miss You all the Time

Miss you all the time....looking long and far
Seeing the distance from my burning eyes
Wondering where you are...
Wasting so much time, remembering soft touches
I wanted you more, than I knew before
Except we found ourselves invariably lost...
In the end it seemed there was no hope for me
I wanted you more, but the great love
That buried us in its sweet lust, wasn't enough anymore....
Missing you more than you knew, with old photographs
Your smell lingering, touching the things that meant the most
Had emptied into us, one at a time... just one at a time...
Tears, anger, through fingertips you slipped
I see you for miles, like a video....dotted with the horizon
So I swim, and breathe and fall by the wayside
And imagine you appearing one day, as you call, my heart stops
Just another day, in paradise...
But you have to know....
Miss you all the time...
In our own short pace
We were so serene
And the world was mine
You held me tight it wasn't a dream.... all the Time

She was Woman

A woman beyond her means
A warrior by day
A lover by night
Fighting each battle
Every day with every breath
She dreamed of marriage
White picket fence
Lots of children
That she would adore
She turned sixteen
Leaving home
Guiding her way
To her new domain
Party life
Lots of fun
Fun turned unto much sun
Moving to Manchester
She became a dancer
Moved through so many lives
She danced through disasters
Through many storms
She was still a little girl deep down inside
Then one night she met a man
They had a love affair
To beat the band
A whirl romance
He got her pregnant
They had a little girl
The little girl looked like her mom
She followed her mom
As she worked two jobs
They were left alone
To fend for themselves
No love in sight, made long nights
The little girl grew up
To watch her mom
Give up on her dreams that made her cry
Then one day as her mom lay dying
The bright young girl
Yelled through tears

I am woman!!!

Brevity Poetry

The Secret
Embarrassed eyes melt,
Confusing my lips with jumbled feelings,
As I whisper 'I love you"

The secret now released;
Forgive the hurt as I ask
To win back your heart

In the Style of T. S. Elliot

The Lonely Tavern
Alone in the dimly lit tavern, smells of old
Dusty of mold, holding glass so cold
Not one spoken word it seems, as dishes clank
Is a mystery of means…

As losing reality that's told
Another day of the lonely road....

Lowest of whispers the party has long ended
Calling time to finally leave
Eyes locked in either direction
Badly falling on their knees
Which the party never leaves...

Lights flicker one times then two
Calm of the realm, offers deafening silence,
With feet stirring across the frontier
Of another night in the lonely tavern
Money spent, pockets empty, one more night alone...

As loners in their homes, warm air of the night
Walking slowly to their icy waters, of fate
Below the harmful word that sows
Stitched in the trees that fright, holding a rather glow
Deep into the forest and many a roads, walking from the tavern
One too many times as the night comes to an end
Another lonely life that brings, sorrow to hearts that long...

This is the day for the lonely

The night was gone, with lonely souls
Prancing around, shattering together
Like anemones secrets, sway of mystics...
Flowing ribbons....that never sway...
Don't let me be lonely...
Caressing dewy skin, blesses me with saving grace
Ripened fruit, dripping lusty color,
Washing away the coral reefs
Under water mating of lips gentle kiss..
Saving grace, don't let me be lonely...
Nowhere to hide
Conjured up a magical side
Passions that were of otherworldly dimensions
Was the saving grace meant to be...
What a day for the lonely...
Quivering heart of celestial lovers
Becoming one with the current,
Erotic maid of blue sea sublime
To the edge of the oceanic dream.....

This is the day for the lonely....

Cries of Confession

As I sit here with years of tears
Traveler of dreams I am
Walking miles alone
Always to roam

Remembering the pain I caused
With the passionate sin that lost
Loves destroyed, never belonging
Always prolonging

Confession to me is hard you see
Never owning up to any belief
One night long ago
It stole my very soul

I hear owls screech, with cries so loud
Or was that me???
Never hearing them speak
Never turning the other cheek

The gun in my hand, seemed to burn
The pain I cannot control
I want the soul deep within
That many years I lost in sin
On this lonely of loneliness
With every door closed
Earth-bed too high, waiting for sleep
Six feet down, my grave is deep
Fingertips deep seated in the dirt
Remembering lives I took
With the gun that shook
In my hand so long ago

This poem was for a contest…
You had to imagine a sin that you possibly had done and got away with it and how life would have been after wards..

Fall Whispers

Perfection is a must
And the leaves fall and the temperature drops
All that glistening about....
The tongue makes music on this fall day
In perfection as she begins to shudder,
Her turbulence a roar
As the leaves fell
Around their loving hearts
Saturated in her waterfall,
He swallows her beauty....
A beautiful soul is she
She flows with flavor
In the autumn bloom
The love that flowed
Made the stars
Roll to move again....

As they move to fall
A paradox of sorts
Wrapped in a cotton blanket
She takes another sip of her cup
As the fall whispers
I am kissing your Dreams...

No One Knows Her Name

Her head bent down, a hole in her chest
Unfulfilled by love that doesn't exist
Her search seems to have no meaning
Wanting so deeply to be hugged
To survive
She is flushed, eyes wet
Teardrops roll her face
Saving everyone to soak her skin
So that she can shed them once again
She cries
Her hair draped around her face
She feels undesirable
Unwanted and losing her reality
Longs to be part of the one she searches for
She waits

Looking in the mirror she disbelieves
As the pitch black of night covers her guiding light
Her search is unworthy of being the one of his dreams
She feels it doesn't matter
She climbs
Still dreaming, even with doubt, or with meaning
Was it truth or falsity?
Wanting the dream to be real
As it fades into the clouds
To die

With head bent down
Dreams gone
Words that don't last
Teas dried up
Lost

No One Knows Her Name

She flies to Nirvana...

She circles the spotlight
Stands before her master
Never to be seen
Sightless behind
The face, she waits...

Holding her breath
Lost,
Overlooking coral reefs darkest seas
Wanting to become one with the current...

Quivering heart
Nothing matters
When the world fades away...

The animal awakens to dawn
Filled days

Stalking her wholeness to feast on
Its tasty morsel from the night before
Puzzles her,
Only to tell its tribal cadence
Draws her forward

Fear overtakes her
With regal grace it swiftly pounces
Cutting her to the realms
Of her kingdom

Submit to your goddess
Surrender your pride
"I possess you now, my beautiful prey"

She flies to Nirvana...

My Dark Lesson

This profound transformation, that I feel right now
Angers me, and destroys the lesson I am trying to learn
There you go hurting all that flows in your way
I fear this bitterness creeping
Enveloping like the plague

Attempting to douse my inner light
Dreams that of my youthful fancies
And shunning those professors
Never belonging, with your hurts and lies

My heart feels like it's been in a turbulent storm, with triggers unknown
Fires flashing and threatening to bury my soul
In perfect bedlam

And there you stand some more, always ready to roam
And hurt again...

With a mute voice, my mind is calling to my phantom
Who are you? Talk to me

My journey now lowers my head, my body gave out
Knowing you will hurt me again.
Trying to adjust

With lips velvet caress licking flames at my waist,
Does not distract from your new, hurtful grip

How many times are you going to hurt my heart?
I feel captive,

And still I stay here while you destroy my life.

I Dream Of You

In twilight's, last chapter
I close my eyes
Gifting myself
Of another dream of you
I am lost in your theater
Every night... after dawn
Crazed... To your addiction of words
I awake alone to my loneliness
One more time...

Holding over to another day, another great
Night of dreams of you,
And the greatest love story ever told...

A Kiss Is Just a Kiss-Un beso es sólo un beso

Un beso es sólo un beso
el día emerge
azorados los vientos
un empuje, un remolcador
todavía conocido
como las alas de una paloma
es tu amor...

Entrecejo arrugado, la confusión crece
lágrimas estallan,
niños que lloran lágrimas han
podido expresar, la consulta...

La sal de un hombre, su nariz molesta
un poco, apenas entre las estrellas
doradas cabelleras su lado
oscuro flores calor en su vientre

un beso los amantes, es sólo un beso
que es un susurro de un soplo de
antaño...
A kiss is Just a Kiss
The day emerges
Flustered winds
A pull, a tug
Still un-known
Like wings on a dove
Is your love....

Creased brow, confusion grows
Tears explode, tears gone
Children cry
Unable to voice, the query ....

The spice of a man, teases her nostrils
A touch, barely there among the stars
Her golden tresses pushed aside
Dark heat blooms in her belly

A lovers kiss, is just a kiss
That's a whisper of a breath
Of days gone by…

Our Hidden Day-oculta en otro día.

Vientos fuertes chillidos
desempolvar tierra látigos
árboles escalofríos y
tormentas furiosas invectivas golpe, rugiente
en órbita
lunar menguante,] gracia
depilación lunas
emitir su hechizo
por favor
ayudarme a encontrar mi camino
entre las tormentas y las lunas canción
oculta en otro día.

Strong winds howl
Dusted earth whips
Trees shiver and blow
Angry storms tirade, bellowing
Orbiting gibbous,
Lunar grace
Waxing moons
Casting your spell
Please
Help me find my way
Among the storms and moons song
In another hidden day..

Debbie

The Note

She slipped a note, stating please no interruptions
Time and place was clear that day
Slipping back and forth filling water
The look he got was sadden of desperation....

The sadness that over took the air between them
She had lots of plans, she said, so please hurry
Tears tore at her eyes, a stiffness in her neck
As the lawyer sat down, with papers in hand.....

He shakes his head in protest words forming in a no
The look she gave him was on the razors edge
He leaned over to her and he whispers,
Pushing napkin to the side, she slid the papers to be signed

No more heart ache, no more lies,
Remembering the wicked games he played
She just knew this would be better,
As she watched his hands shake again...

She stood up looking one last time
At the man she loved
He knew that look as he remember the bride he had lost
His ears hear the whirl of dishes clanking...

You Don't Always Have to Love Me

Currents push through me, seeping out my pores
Not a whisper of space as I trace your face
Your body completely surrounds, oh yes I want more
Floating back to a place more real
I remember now, it's only a dream
Simply collecting facets, of me piece by piece
As the deepest breath surrounds
Entangling every breath,
Like falling grains, through an hour glass immortal;
Doubts are wisp away into forgotten shadows
Not a single word was said, dancing around their love
Carried along the current of a quiet melody, she said
'You don't always have to love me'....

Secret Hollow

Silence embodies as I walk, through this cave...at a glance
In a midst of times paradox, I soak in the quiet all about me
My eyes wide open in my ancient dreams
I wonder where this will lead....

Fireflies dance,
Talons of the sacred guru, embrace my spirit
Of my inner child..

I touch the dampness that surrounds my life
Longing to escape these stone walls
Where my inner light has mirrored
Through foggy separation

I am a branded child, in this secret hollow...

Let the Sun Set

Schooled now with certain desires, hostile lessons
Burning flames...

This profound transformation holds me to the spot
And angers me...

Leave me to my dreams, the powerful on-slaughter of humanity
Wasted away from my cocooned, protection..

I don't want to hear any more..

I want my youthful fancies, my short shirts and long hair,
Dancing my life away....
My inner light protests, wants more.
Searching for the tiny seed, within the walls of my soul,
Flirting on the edge of my fingers..
Waiting just waiting...
Cocooning my panic, waiting for the warm embrace,
And maybe just maybe..

Holding on to this fragile threaded life, thoughts of home carry me forward...

Awaiting safety...

Tortured

I sit within my grave forsaken all purity
Crossroads for lost souls as my vamped spirit cries
Cold damp earth is my blanket where dreams of my lover is unbound
That brings forth my darkened soul....

Spirit speaks to me, nightmares visit me
You penetrate my darkened life
Suffering, with half desire
These feeling have been thrown away
To vanquish eternally, knowing I should die...

I hand over myself to you with a bleeding heart
I have liked many, I have loved few
But none as such as the love I have for you...

I ceased to be no more, as this tortured soul...

Two Hearts Two Rings...Are Wed

Love to be... this earth captures heavenly spirits of thee
Rested on their highest praise of all
That keeps the heart of gold....of the united couple so glorious
Their light of celestial mansions created in the design of their hearts...

Doors of heaven are covered by her veil of loveliness
Love inspiring the beauty of it all
Their brilliance of the stars, how glorious
Sun's rays stir and draw light above their pass-ways, this night..

The sun shines on the wedding, glorifying their union
With the moving rays of God
Blessed are those that come before Him and profess their love
That lays the foundation of miracles, where garments of gentle breath....

Fountains of love overflowing, as they profess so much
Their grace are exalted and born of blazing spiritual fire
Founded in their many triumphs of a thousand blessings
Let the sun set and the moonshine over this Holy Communion...

Two Hearts and two rings are wed this day...

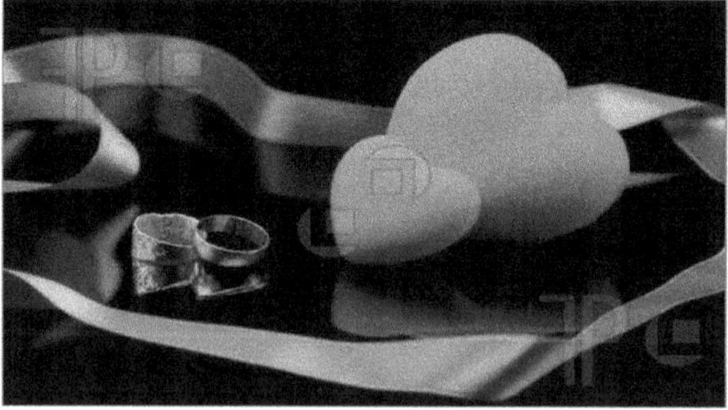

Shadow Land of Heaven

Through the shadow lands of paradise
A dream seeker that I am
My inner world finds my inner peace
Where life shines and water gives life
I find my stairway to heaven this very day....

A butterfly glides through the heavenly orange bias
Within the circles of true life motion
A processing light takes hold of my eyes
Leads me to the narrow light....

Face to face with my tarnished soul
A light rain covers my face
My tears stream my vision
I hold my breath one last time
As I face the angel of death....

Her Red Ribbon

Her red ribbon lay on the floor as tears fill his eyes
How she had loved him, as he had adored
So many times before she wore that red ribbon
That he gave her long time ago
Falling with her roses as they drifted below...

Lying in bed and floating away
The morning breaks with a sound of a soft angel voice
It's time to say goodbye, as her hand slips to the floor
Her smudged lipstick with a solace of grace
Smiled a smile that would be no more...

She lay on her bed of glory one last time
And he sat with tears falling like rain
Her hand so frail from hard life past
His heart drops and cries so loud,
As she takes her last breathe....

Her red ribbon, silent on the floor...

Seeking

Seeking out your existence
Wavering on a breeze
I master my courage
As I tell you my sorrow....

I will wish the impossible
Seeking out your existence
I master my courage
Completely in reverse....Still seeking...

As I master my courage, my mind screams
Wavering on a breeze
This is simply not me
As I tell you my sorrow...

Screaming Out Our Names

As we scream out our names
We go insane
What next our souls
How do we ever know?

Screaming is the rule,
Mighty one that's a fool
Mouth wide open
Eyes are mighty shut...

Tears won't come
The warm air turns cold
Fire still blooms
Tasting, their existence to be
Nevermore

Hearts will stop
Strength lets go
Masters quit dancing
Nails bite the palm....

As we scream out our names

Our Twilights Last Chapter

I close my eyes
Whispers I hear as she walks by
You sit there so still, as I cry....
She has reached inside of you
She caress your words your touch that's gone....

My body aching to feel you
Entwined within my own mind....

My empty hand that yearns
With another dream of you

Just a fortnight ago, we strove the avenue
Hands linked of paired, our wandering souls...

We halted beneath the brightest moon
You were my fantasy...

I raise high on the drug of your whispering lines
Never seeking sobriety, for this rousing affliction...

My Love My Life

My Love The curtain descended on the show
At last the cast took a bow

There you were reaching for the stars
My heart you took in your hands that night

You reached for my hand so new
Took my life into yours I knew

You told me life was a song
You kissed my breeze all day long

You were my life and love in a sweet melody
We danced into the night

One last time has come as we gather round
All those unforgotten days so lost

Fond memories brought moments of sob'
Hurting my heart never to be.... I knew it the moment
Again after years of disappointment

Don't go I cry, my eyes gone dry
A hint of goodbye just one more time

This crying for my love my life
I didn't mind the whirl
One last times my love we gather here...

You are and have been my perfect love....
My Life

Nick Are You there?

Hello my sweet man,
My heart you hold
My words be told
Of moonlight nights
Kisses and more
We made music
That we didn't regret....

Our hearts
Rang out in rhythm with each kiss...

What happened can I help
You are down and out
I am here by your side...

What do you say?
They are waiting for stage call
As you fly out to bow
As you throw me your love
With every drop of rain
Good bye my sweet man,
You used to visit every night
We would play to our delight
With each morning doubtful plight

I send you my hellos
It seems so long ago
I know she is with you now
So it's time to say 'goodbye...

But if there is anything I can do
You know where to find me, my love...

My Love Beacon

Hello you
I am curious to see how your heart
Is holding up
Seeing you standing there
Looking so good, my Dear friend
My tears I hide, my longing thrives
The sound I hear is your kindness
It was the purest love, you gave
Turning the wheel
Divine blessings
Of a thousand high souls, I hide
With a million drops of you
Falling like rain between my life
Like rays of midnight sun.....
Millions of drops of you, my friend
Falling all around my body so
Kissing my sound so blue
Holding the side of light
Sweet stars so bright
Of the millions of drops of rain
That falls on our bodies
As kisses explore, all in my mind
The image forward, I wish I could explore...
I dream of you!!

Remembering You

As my whole world turns
Colors of grayish blue
Lonely days
That came from
The never ending, loving you...

As I remember...

Days slowly turn to years
With every faint echo
Hundreds of vivid memories
Tireless supporter, leaning on stone pillar

And I remember too...

Tears sliding down my face
One last time
Haunted by old recurrences
Holding comfort in...
With rugs full of rips and tears

One last time
Remembering you

Candlelight

Million candles
Flow in the room that makes it glow
Drifting as lilies
That holds
Secrets
I reach to the walls
Shadows laugh
I fear the pain
The blood that tickles
Through the rain
The pain

Candlelight
Brings no shame

Truth sings in a empty hall
As a whisper of a cool breeze
All lined with purple....

Please defend our souls,
I will fight to make us whole...

This Is the End

I climbed on board, prepared to hoist my sails
But all I found...

Misery bound, don't know what to say
My heart and body are dying
How can I be so alone on these deserted sands.....

Looking out beyond the shores
Sun goes down, darkness creeps in
And still I am not sound...

Writing this end... on this piece of paper
As it pauses at my feet and rolls
Moving quickly between worlds
On this silent stance, that could be my last
Please come find my bones, and send them to my lost lover
The gentle rocking of the coming waves
As I throw my body to the horizon where the dolphins play....

We Ran Happy

Summer cupped us
Hot mouths to feed
Drank our vodka
Said ' I love you'
With laughter we counted
The fire ants
Crazy days of smoking weed
Our sweat like beads of rain
We were invisible with the fireflies
We ran happy...

End of Feeling Says You

Worlds collide on separate planes
As the werewolf roams all night

Emotions left behind
As he doesn't understand

The hunger folds into his soul
Separate from human rights
Minds fill with uncertain fear...and begin the horrible fight...

Stalking the soul like ashes on the roaming sea
Depression sets in as the soul knows
Limitless begins in blood thirsty drops
End of feeling, lifeless minutes... Says you

As the werewolf feeds once more...

This is for a contest on all poetry.com

Poetry Found

Writing in my heart
Walking to my pen
Dreams following me
Heartbreak does declare
Being lost and being found
In my poetry... on my lonely street
I am somebody and someone cares
My pens flows to my eyes, heart cry to my soul
Still on this lonely street with pen in one hand
Bottle in the other
I stand....

Lord My Attention

Watching a snowball roll
As it picks up speed, it began to grow
Then its big and powerful like YOU...

Even if YOU are silent

The more you love and share God's love
The more love you get back
The longer we share
The more capacity we have to know
If you want more then try giving it away
Lord, my desire is to have, all the love you got...

Oh what a gift. What a dept. of Love
Lord your voice, my desire
Your free gift, I give you me....

I am filled,
With your unexpected and undeserved love
Lord you have my attention.....Even if YOU are silent...
Love Debbie

The

End

Reviews

Author and poet Deborah Brooks Langford
What can I say about Deborah Brooks Langford?
She is an awesome talent who writes from the heart.
She is constantly writing unique and heartfelt poetry.
She is a never ending talent and she touches the heart with her work.
She has the most giving heart and is always thinking of what she can do to help others.
She is my friend, a joy to my heart and I am so very much honored to know her.
Poet Gina Joy Bennett

Deborah Brooks Langford,
A wonderful poet with the grace of a dove,
She writes with a heart full of Jesus Christ's love.
She is sensitive and dear to many who seek refuge in words to inspire and thoughts to impress.
Struck by the arrow of Cupid but still standing
She has never allowed anyone to tear her down.
Her beliefs are firm but not demanding.
I encourage everyone to read her all of her lovely books.
And be encouraged by the ones that she knows who can cook!
Thank you, Deborah for sharing your heart.
I can't wait to read your next book.
So when can I start?
A review of Deborah Brooks Langford, my most favorite author and poet,
By Author and Poet Christina M. Castro

Author and Poet Deborah Brooks Langford
It is a great joy to read her wonderful poems
She has a stunning writing style
I was simply amazed how creative and talented she is
Her poetry touches the heart and soul of her readers
Each verse is a woven tapestry of magic
Which captivates the heart with an overflow of emotions
Its music that soothes the inter spirit
Deborah Brooks Langford is a very talented poet and writer
Who is compassionate and caring…
By: Author and Poet Shirley Denton

Debbie Brooks Langford, Author and Poetess
I have during the last year had the advantage of getting
To know the author Debbie Brooks Langford, both as
A friend and also by her writings
I have been very impressed over her language especially in
Her poetry, which shows so much of a personality
With a great heart and a sensitiveness, not so common
In our society of today
She stands for beauty, for love, and for kind relations
Between friends and family
Her prose is vivid and warm-hearted, describing much of
Her own rich life and her experiences are shared with us
As cream on the cake
I can with all of my heart recommend her great poetry and
Her prose and I am so thankful for all she has given to me
As a friend and also as a poet and writer
Many thanks dear Debbie Brooks Langford
And Good Luck in the future.
Kerstin Centerwall Author/Poetess

Books By
Deborah Brooks Langford

Cookbooks

Cooking the World Over
http://www.lulu.com/shop/deborah-brooks-langford/cooking-the-world-over/paperback/product-21220158.html

Poets' Recipes from the Heart
http://www.lulu.com/shop/deborah-brooks-langford/poets-recipes-from-the-heart/paperback/product-21254796.html

Poetry Books

My Heart I Give
ttp://www.lulu.com/shop/deborah-brooks-langford/my-heart-i-give/paperback/product-21297560.html

Silenced Hearts
ttp://www.lulu.com/shop/deborah-brooks-langford/silenced-hearts/paperback/product-21295956.html

Break of a new Dawn
http://www.lulu.com/shop/deborah-brooks-langford/break-of-a-new-dawn/paperback/product-2114977 8.html

One Day Soon
http://www.lulu.com/shop/deborah-brooks-langford/one-day-soon/paperback/product-21193967.html

Novel

Brooke
http://www.lulu.com/shop/deborah-brooks-langford/brooke/paperback/product-21199975.html

Author and Poet Deborah Brooks Langford

hen I was in 5th grade my teacher introduced me to books. Jane Eyre withering heights... etc... I fell in love with books... They took me on adventures and I would daydream... And I started writing...
have been writing poems all my life. When I was in school I would write instead of listen and dream of different poems and stories. My passion is poetry. I love to write and if I don't write I feel very depressed. Writing my poetry and stories helps me emotionally.
I was born in North Carolina, I am a military brat. We lived in Germany and Spain and Turkey. My father's side of the family comes from Cherokee North Carolina and my mother's families are English.
ledicated everything I do in the memory of my wonderful sweet mother and to Jesus Christ My Lord and Savior.
I have written two poetry books.
"My Heart I give"
"Silenced Hearts"
"Break of a New Dawn"
"One Day Soon"
Plus, my new Novel "Brooke".
The sequel to "BROOKE", IS "BROOKE AND NICK". It is almost finished...
And the third book in the series. "Forever Brooke" is
Brooke in her younger days
I am working on children's books too. Nine in all.....
I have two cookbooks published
"Cooking the World Over"......
"Poets recipes From the Heart"
I love working for our country. I am very passionate about that. I love working with the veterans. My ther was a veteran from Pork chop in the Korean War and two tours in Vietnam. My Father Sgt. Bill I call him went on to be with the Lord this past June 2013 where he joined my mother.
I married my sweet husband from high school, He retired from the Navy.

Deborah Brooks Langford
D2WP

www.ingramcontent.com/pod-product-compliance
Ingram Content Group UK Ltd.
Pitfield, Milton Keynes, MK11 3LW, UK
UKHW012254240726
13966UKWH00004B/1414